VICTORIOUS
MINDSET

30 Day Devotional

SARAH MALANOWSKI

Victorious Mindset, Second Edition
Copyright 2015, 2025 by Sarah Malanowski. All rights reserved.

PUBLISHER: Shine Press
4522 W. Village Dr. #1294 Tampa Florida 34624
Shine-Press.com | Jodi@Shine-Press.com

No part of this publication may be reproduced, stored in a retrieval system or transmitted in any way by any means, electronic, mechanical, photocopy, recording or otherwise without the prior permission of the author except as provided by USA copyright law.

Scripture quotations marked (AMP) are taken from the *Amplified Bible*, Copyright © 1954, 1958, 1962, 1964, 1965, 1987 by The Lockman Foundation. Used by permission.

Scripture quotations marked (KJV) are taken from the *King James Version*. Cambridge Edition: 1769; King James Bible Online, 2023.

Scripture quotations marked (MSG) are taken from *The Message*. Copyright © 1993, 1994, 1995, 1996, 2000, 2001, 2002. Used by permission of NavPress Publishing Group.

The Holy Bible: New International Version: Containing The Old Testament and the New Testament. (1984). International Bible Society. All scripture references are (NIV84) unless otherwise noted. .

Scripture quotations marked (NKJV) are taken from the *New King James Version*. Copyright © 1982 by Thomas Nelson, Inc. Used by permission. All rights reserved.

Cover and book interior design by Sondra Howe

Published in the United States of America
ISBN: 978-1-947066-19-9

1. HEATH & FITNESS / Mental Health
2. RELIGION / Christian Living / Spiritual Growth 15.01.09

Endorsement for
Victorious Mindset

"As a Chiropractor, I have encouraged and guided thousands of patients back to health. The one common thread among all who have reversed disease and transformed their lives has been a *victorious mindset*. With pinpoint accuracy, Sarah has addressed the one key ingredient by which everything in life rises and falls: your mind or a mind set on Christ."

—Dr. Raul Serrano
Ignite Chiropractic & Wellness

Dedicated to . . .

- **God** for being my number one and teaching me what it means to have a *Victorious Mindset*. You have equipped me to be a true overcomer!

- **Paul**, for reminding me that writing is a gift and God wants me to use it for His glory. For supporting me in my writing dreams and often doing whatever it takes to make them a reality.

- **Zion**, for your strength and the way you hold me accountable for what I say. You are an incredible young man, and I am proud to be your mom.

- **Gabriel**, for reminding me to slow down and just savor the moments. You amaze me with your eye for detail and ability to create just about anything.

> *Do not conform any longer to the*
> *pattern of this world,*
> *but be transformed by*
> *the renewing of your mind.*
> *Then you will be able to test and approve*
> *what God's will is—*
> *His good, pleasing and perfect will.*
>
> —ROMANS 12:2

CONTENTS

Foreword	8
Introduction	10
Day 1: Transformation Begins in the Mind	14
Day 2: Mindful Heart	16
Day 3: Heavenly Mindset	18
Day 4: Humble Mindset	20
Day 5: Mindful Reset	22
Day 6: Enjoy the Journey	24
Day 7: Thoughts to Reject	26
Day 8: Mind on the Prize	28
Day 9: Victorious Mindset	32
Day 10: Mindfully Moving Forward	36
Day 11: Faith Minded	38
Day 12: Childlike Mindset	40
Day 13: Resisting the Devil	42
Day 14: Drawing Near to God	44
Day 15: Dealing with Distractions	46
Day 16: No Worries	50
Day 17: Swan-Like Attitude	52
Day 18: Plan of Action	54
Day 19: Living Complete	56

Day 20: The Complete Life	58
Day 21: Sharpened by the Word	62
Day 22: Worry Free	64
Day 23: God's View on Life	66
Day 24: Thought Inventory	70
Day 25: Captive for Christ	72
Day 26: Peace of Mind	74
Day 27: Handing over the Paintbrush	76
Day 28: No One Loves You More	78
Day 29: Lavished on Me	80
Day 30: Victory or Defeat	84
Bibliography	86
About the Author	89

FOREWORD

Renewing the mind involves the lining up of our thinking with God's truth each day. Sarah's new devotional book, *Victorious Mindset*, is a fine tool for doing just that. Each daily reading blends Bible verses, prayers, classic quotes from spiritual giants, as well as stories, reflections, analogies, and insights that could only have come from personal times with the Savior, Jesus.

I was amazed that Sarah gravitated toward verse after verse that has also led to transformation and victory in my own life. Whether facing discouragement, battle, temptation, or even if walking with God in fellowship, confidence, and strength, there is an encouragement for every reader.

Sarah's thoughts are simple enough to grasp, yet deep enough to grip one's heart and mind. She has not merely placed words on a page, but has expressed lessons from the crucible of her life and those that have come from study and meditation and from ruminating on each morsel of the Word. As one of the pastors of the local church where Sarah serves and worships, my appreciation of her writing has been increased as I have seen a bit of her faith lived out. I have been in the position to observe the trust in the Lord that she and her husband, Paul, displayed with joy and courage as they faced disappointment and pain in at least one of life's difficult challenges. She has learned to pray, "Help me to enjoy the journey today and be less concerned about the destination" (Day 6).

Truly, Sarah inspires the cultivating of a godly mindset. She has proclaimed the necessity and blessing of the mind yielded to the Spirit (Romans 8:5–6) and recognizes that the believer, as a new person in Christ, "*is being renewed in knowledge in the image of its Creator*" (Colossians 3:10b).

I pray that you will walk in victory as you adjust your daily thinking and believing to the truth of God's Word. May this devotional work assist you in praying in agreement with David; "*You will fill me with joy in Your presence*" (Psalm 16:11b).

—Greg Murphy
MINISTER—FAMILY CARE
Idlewild Baptist Church in Tampa (Lutz), Florida

INTRODUCTION

Recently, I had a great opportunity to put the words of this book into practice. My family and I were on our way to enjoy a beautiful vacation. I had brought my computer to do the final edits of this book. We stopped to reminisce a little bit at a beach my husband spent time at as a child. We made some great new memories as we watched my son play in the sand and enjoy the water.

After dinner, we headed back to our car only to find out that we had been robbed. My husband's suitcase had been stolen, which contained our passports for the cruise we were about to embark on, his belongings for the trip, and quite a few other things. He was left with only the clothes on his back. I also noticed that my computer had been stolen along with my book files.

I can't come close to explaining how hurt, angry, and frustrated I was in that moment. Satan went to work on my mind immediately. I felt stupid. Why would I leave such an expensive item in the car? I felt violated. Who would do something like this to a family headed out on vacation? I felt angry. How much time was it going to take to unravel this terrible mess?

Even as I thought these thoughts, the Holy Spirit whispered to me the very words I wrote in this book and my *Joyful Living* book. I was given a choice. A choice to dwell on what went wrong. A choice to entertain the thoughts of my enemy. A choice to wallow in my pain. The choice was always mine. Immediately, I spoke Scripture to myself saying "The joy of the Lord is my strength" (Nehemiah 8:10).

I took time to go back to the verses I've memorized and did my best to dwell on the Truth of God.

God was teaching me in that moment how to have a *Victorious Mindset*. This mindset doesn't always come easy, and sometimes it comes at a cost. Every day I'm at the bottom of the mindset mountain having to make my climb to the top once again. I scale the heights and desire to ascend to the top. It's a tough climb and sometimes it feels like my hands are bleeding as I cling to God's Truth with all my might. I dig my nails in and set out every day to be victorious.

There are moments of anguish, moments of pain, moments of sheer desperation, and moments of frustration. But during my fight to get up this mindset mountain, I also experience moments of triumph. Having a *Victorious Mindset* will always take work. It does not come easy. In this I'm reminded of the words Jesus spoke in Luke 9:23.

> *Then He said to them all: "If anyone would come after Me, he must deny himself and take up his cross daily and follow me."*

Jesus calls us to take up our cross daily and follow Him. The only way to be victorious is to keep Christ at the forefront of our minds every day.

Henry Ford once said, *"Whether you think you can, or you think you can't—you're right."* Everything we accomplish in life starts with this mindset. The greatest victories we experience in life start with a mind set on the things of Christ. The best way to do this is to do a daily study of God's Word, meditate on the Truth, and memorize as much of Scripture as we possibly can. The only way to fight the continual lies of the enemy is to feed daily on God's Truth.

I have chosen the way of truth; I have set my heart on Your laws. I hold fast to Your statutes, O Lord; do not let me be put to shame. I run in the path of Your commands, for You have set my heart free. (PSALM 119:30–32)

My prayer is that this thirty-day devotional will make the climb up the *Victorious Mindset* mountain a little easier and that you will experience more moments of triumph. May you continue to find joy in the Lord, may your mind be used for His glory, and may you find yourself living the victorious life in Christ!

Let's go scale this mountain together,

Sarah

P. S. It is tempting to change this introduction to current circumstances I've walked through but as I read it I'm reminded that every step in God's direction stretches and develops my spiritual muscles to scale the heights like never before. So, for the sake of this book and the time frame in which it was originally written, I will keep everything as is from the first edition. Only slight changes. It will be groundwork for future material I create on having a victorious life in Jesus. Stay tuned for some good books to come with plenty of new life stories from which to draw!

SET

YOUR MINDS ON THINGS *above*

NOT ON *earthly* THINGS

Coloss. 3:2

Day 1

TRANSFORMATION BEGINS IN THE MIND

Do not conform any longer to the pattern of this world, but be transformed by the renewing of your mind. Then you will be able to test and approve what God's will is—His good, pleasing and perfect will.

—ROMANS 12:2

Live It Out

The transformation of our lives begins in the mind. We cannot fully be devoted to God until we transform the way we think. The Bible calls us to take every thought captive and make it obedient to Christ (2 Cor. 10:5), to set our minds on things above not on earthly things (Col. 3:2), and to think things that are true, noble, right, pure, lovely, admirable, excellent, and praise-worthy (Phil. 4:8).

Does your mind need to go through a transformation? I know my mind daily has to be renewed by God's Word. There is only one thing on this earth that can renew the way you think and that's the Word of God. The Word of God has the power to be living and active in your life (Heb. 4:12). It can cut through every thought that does not bring God glory. I challenge you to take time in God's

Word. Daily renew your mind by meditating on God's Truth. Allow God's Truth to take root in your life and change the way you think.

When your mind is renewed by the Word, then and only then, will you be able to test and approve what God's will is for your life. God's will is good, pleasing, and perfect. He has an amazing plan for your life, but you need to get into the Word to find out what that is. Don't let another day go by without getting into God's Truth and finding out what He has for you there.

I have hidden Your word in my heart that I might not sin against You.

—PSALM 119:11

Pray It Through

Lord, please show me where I'm conforming to the patterns of this world. Please transform the way I think. Renew my mind and help me walk more uprightly before You. May Your Word be hidden in my heart so that I can test and approve what Your will is for my life. I know that Your will is good, pleasing, and perfect. I desire to follow you completely!

> *Knowledge is indispensable to Christian life and service. If we do not use the mind that God has given us, we condemn ourselves to spiritual superficiality and cut ourselves off from many of the riches of God's grace.*
>
> —JOHN STOTT

Day 2

MINDFUL HEART

Since, then, you have been raised with Christ, set your hearts on things above, where Christ is seated at the right hand of God.

—COLOSSIANS 3:1

Live It Out

Lately, God is reminding me to be focused on things that are eternal. This stuff down here on earth is really just a glimpse of what is to come. I can't get my heart entangled in things that don't last forever. God has called me to set my heart on Him.

Inside our hearts lie the intentions, the desires, the emotions, and the passions that drive us forward. Our happiness, sadness, love, and mercy all exist within our heart. The motivation to succeed in life begins at the core of our heart. God calls us to set the things in our hearts on Him. He calls us to align our emotions, desires, and intentions with His heart for us.

Are we loving others like God loves them? Are we forgiving others like God forgives them? Do our desires line up with His Word? It's so easy to get wrapped up in the things on this earth that just don't matter. But God has called us to a standard where our hearts are to be set on Him. His standard calls us to so much more than this world can offer. I'm tired of being distracted by the world's meaningless toys and temporary satisfaction. I want the things of God that truly satisfy, the things that last, the things that can heal my heart and help me become more like Christ. Do you want this too?

But if from there you seek the Lord your God, you will find Him if you look for Him with all your heart and with all your soul.

—DEUTERONOMY 4:29

Pray It Through

Lord, I desire to seek You with all my heart. I pray that I will be steadfast and invincible when it comes to searching out the things of Your heart. May I not grow weary of doing right by You, but may I daily be renewed so that I may bring You glory!

If you live gladly to make others glad in God, your life will be hard, your risks will be high, and your joy will be full.
—JOHN PIPER

Day 3

HEAVENLY MINDSET

Set your minds on things above, not on earthly things.
—COLOSSIANS 3:2

Live It Out

The mind is where decisions are made, a place where thoughts are given life, the place where doubt can seep in, the place where logic and reasoning fight for the right answer, the place where understanding is formed, and the place where wisdom is developed. The mind developed in Christ is a powerful tool.

Is your mind developed in the things of God? There is an easy test to find out. Simply, walk through this next verse and ask yourself if this describes your thoughts.

Finally, brothers, whatever is true, whatever is noble, whatever is right, whatever is pure, whatever is lovely, whatever is admirable—if anything is excellent or praiseworthy—think about such things.

—PHILIPPIANS 4:8

Did you pass the test? Are your thoughts true, noble, right, pure, lovely and admirable? If not, seek the Lord and ask Him to transform your thoughts. May your thoughts line up with His Word, so that your mind can be a tool for God's kingdom!

VICTORIOUS MINDSET | DAY 3

Pray It Through

Dear Father God, I set my heart on Your desires for me. I pray that You will continue to adjust my attitude, my behavior, and my desires to please You. May my mind continue to be transformed by Your Word and may I learn how to focus on thoughts that are pure, lovely, right, true, and excellent. May my thoughts reflect the glory of Your Son as I walk out my day today!

> *The Christian mind is the prerequisite of Christian thinking, and Christian thinking is the prerequisite for Christian action.*
> —HARRY BLAMIRES

Day 4

HUMBLE MINDSET

For by the grace given me I say to every one of you, Do not think of yourself more highly than you ought, but rather think of yourself with sober judgment, in accordance with the measure of faith God has given you.

—ROMANS 12:3

Live It Out

This verse reminds us that there is no place for inflated pride in the believer's life. It's pretty easy to get caught up in who we are when we compare ourselves to others. We love to come out ahead and think that at least we are a little better than so and so. But the truth is, it's only by the grace of God that anyone of us has anything good to show for. We must compare ourselves to Jesus and not to each other. Jesus is the perfect standard! And I can tell you that every time I compare myself to Him—I am humbled! I have a long way to go!

Humble yourselves, therefore, under God's mighty hand, that He may lift you up in due time.

—1 PETER 5:6

When we choose to humble ourselves before the Lord…He promises to lift us up. It may not be today; it may not be tomorrow. But God promises to lift the humble up in due time.

VICTORIOUS MINDSET | DAY 4

Humble yourselves before the Lord, and He will lift you up.
—JAMES 4:10

Pray It Through

Dear Father God, Please give me a humble spirit before You. May my attitude be pleasing in your sight. I pray that I will humble myself before You on a daily basis and wait for You to lift me up in due time. Lord, may my life be completely surrendered to You and may I use my talents to edify the Body of Christ.

> *True humility is not thinking less of yourself; it is thinking of yourself less.*
> —C. S. LEWIS

Day 5

MINDFUL REST

Because of the Lord's great love we are not consumed, for His compassions never fail. They are new every morning; great is Your faithfulness.

—LAMENTATIONS 3:22–23

Live It Out

Do you ever wish you could go back in your life and take back a moment? Maybe you wish you could press the Reset button and just start over. Have you ever wished you could just click your heels together like Dorothy did in *The Wizard of Oz* and just wake up out of your dream? Do you look back on life and see places where you could have, should have, or would have done better? Unfortunately, the answer to these questions is all too often yes. Many people want to take back a moment. Many want to press the Reset button. Some just want to click their heels and wake up out of a dream. Then there are others who live on the "woulda, coulda, shoulda" philosophy!

There is good and bad news for you! I'll give you the bad news first. Yesterday is gone! There is nothing you can do about it. You can't take back what happened, and you can't change it. However, the good news is, today is a new day. And just like the passage above says "new every morning," so also we should not be focusing on yesterday's mistakes.

VICTORIOUS MINDSET | DAY 5

God has something new for today. Take what came from yesterday and learn from it; let it mold your character and shape who you will become for tomorrow. Don't miss another moment of today in wasted thoughts of yesterday!

Those who live according to the sinful nature have their minds set on what that nature desires; but those who live in accordance with the Spirit have their minds set on what the Spirit desires. The mind of sinful man is death, but the mind controlled by the Spirit is life and peace.

—ROMANS 8:5-6

Pray It Through

Lord, I pray that my mind will be renewed by Your Spirit today. May the Holy Spirit control my mind and teach me how to better follow You. I long to experience the life and peace You offer on a daily basis.

Life is 10% what happens to you and 90% how you react to it.

—CHARLES R. SWINDOLL

Day 6

ENJOY THE JOURNEY

We are assured and know that [God being a partner in their labor] all things work together and are [fitting into a plan] for good to and for those who love God and are called according to [His] design and purpose.

—ROMANS 8:28 (AMP)

Live It Out

How many things work together for God's good? *All things!* God doesn't leave anything out. Yes, we may not understand the meaning of what is going on at the time, but God knows and He will work it out for good. We are all too often about the destination in life, when God is all about the journey.

In fact, I think about my little niece and nephew who came to visit me a few years ago with my sister and brother-in-law. This was a big trip for them in the car from Minnesota to Florida. They did not fully understand the length of time it would take to get from Minnesota to Florida. They just knew they were coming. They had to trust their parents to get here. We often forget that God is driving. He knows the way, and sometimes, even though it doesn't make much sense that it's taking so long to get to our destination, we still need to trust that He has our best interest in mind. He has not forgotten us.

Today, choose to enjoy the journey! Let go of your questions and concerns. Trust in God's perfect timing, and know that He is working all things together for your good!

> *The Lord appeared to us in the past, saying; "I have loved you with an everlasting love; I have drawn you with lovingkindness."*
>
> —JEREMIAH 31:3

Pray It Through

Dear Father God, please help me to never forget that all the details of my life are in Your hands. Help me to enjoy the journey today and be less concerned about the destination. May Your everlasting love comfort me and draw me close. May it draw me away from my current mindset and help me focus my heart's steps on You!

Prayer is not so much an act as it is an attitude—an attitude of dependency, dependency upon God.
—A. W. PINK

Day 7

THOUGHTS TO REJECT

Therefore, there is now no condemnation for those who are in Christ Jesus.

—ROMANS 8:1

Live It Out

A huge thing to remember is to never be afraid to press the Reject button! The reject button is very useful during times of negativity. Reject any thought of the enemy that does not line up with God's Word. Never allow a thought of anxiety, fear, or condemnation to take root in your mind. Every negative thought that you dwell on will keep you paralyzed and ineffective when it comes to walking out your faith. It is so important to freely press the reject button when thoughts of doubt seep in.

The next time you hear one of these thoughts… "You're not good enough, You don't have what it takes, You can't possibly make it, You're not a good enough Christian, You should have done things better, etc." Press the "reject button." Don't even allow your mind to accept the falsehood of these sayings. You are a child of God! Take ownership of that. Rise up! Listen to the Truth, accept the Truth and reject the lies! Reject the guilt and condemnation.

VICTORIOUS MINDSET | DAY 7

I have told you these things, so that in Me you may have peace. In this world you will have trouble. But take heart! I have overcome the world.

—JOHN 16:33

Pray It Through

Dear Lord, please help me reject every thought of the enemy today. May I not accept anything less than Your best for my mind. May I dwell on things that are true, lovely, noble, and right. May my mind be used for Your glory!

Vision is the ability to see God's presence, to perceive God's power, to focus on God's plan in spite of the obstacles.
—CHARLES R. SWINDOLL

Day 8

MIND ON THE PRIZE

Do you not know that in a race all the runners run, but only one gets the prize? Run in such a way as to get the prize.
—1 CORINTHIANS 9:24

Here is a simple prayer to help you get a better mindset on the things of Christ. God gave me this prayer during a time of searching after the things of His heart for my life.

Pray It Through

Dear Father God, lately, I have been thinking a lot about my spiritual race. Where am I at on this race? Am I running with everything I've got? Is there any sin that holds me back from fully running for You? I see that I have the ability to throw off every sin and everything that would try so easily to entangle me (Heb. 12:1–2). Lord, that's what I choose to do. I choose to throw off every sin. I want to rid myself of the baggage I carry.

I lay my sins at the foot of the cross. I lay down my pride and pray that You will humble me in Your sight. I pray that I will decrease every day so that You can increase in me. May my life be more about you than anything else! God, help me to serve You with my talents and my gifts. Help me not to take for granted all that I've been given. Lord, I want to run. I want to run hard after You! I want to give You my all because You deserve my all. I want my moments every day to matter.

Lord, You know my heart. You know where I fall and where I need Your help to get back up. You know what weighs heavy on my mind. You know the aches in my heart. You know the needs that surround me. You know every pain and every joy. You know where my thoughts went today. You know what things I said that weren't honoring to you. You know the times today when I did not serve you to the best of my ability. God, please help me to do better tomorrow. Help me to do better even in this next minute!

I want my days to be filled with one less judgmental thought, one less careless word, one less disobedient moment, one less prideful moment, one less disagreement, one less moment of unforgiveness, one less moment of anxiety, one less moment of fear, one less moment of resentment, one less moment of greed, one less moment of impatience, and one less moment of self-promotion. I want my life to be filled with moments where I understand Your grace and sin less because of it. I know that I will never be sinless on this earth, but I do feel that I can sin less every day. God, I want to strive to be more like Your Son! I want to reflect His image in everything I do, say, and think. God, I want You to be glorified in me.

Please melt away every ounce of me and help me to be a better reflection of Your Word. May it be Your Truth that seeps out of my being, may it be your words that proceed from my mouth, may it be Your heart of love that comes alive in me, and may it be Your purpose that prevails in my life!

VICTORIOUS MINDSET | DAY 8

Abba Father, I thank You for hearing my prayer and for being Lord over my life. May every step I take in this race be honoring to You. Please help me to run my race well, so that I can one day say, "I have fought the good fight, I have finished the race, I have kept the faith" (2 Tim. 1:7). Help me fight the good fight, to finish the race, and to keep the faith. I'm all in! I'm longing for the eternal prize that You have set aside for me in glory. May I never lose sight of You and all that You have for me!

Live as though Christ died yesterday, rose from the grave today, and is coming back tomorrow.
—THEODORE EPP

You keep him in perfect peace whose mind is stayed on you, because he trusts in you

······ ISAIAH 26:3 ······

VICTORIOUS MINDSET

The mind of sinful man is death, but the mind controlled by the Spirit is life and peace.

—ROMANS 8:6

Live It Out

I want to share my top five secrets to a victorious mindset in Christ. I pray that you will put them into practice and find victory in your current situation. May God use the circumstances of your current trial to draw you ever closer to Himself!

1. *Study the Word of God.* Nothing can give you a more victorious mindset than the Word of God. God's Word will refresh you, strengthen you, and renew your hope on a daily basis!

> *For the Word of God is living and active. Sharper than any double-edged sword, it penetrates even to dividing soul and spirit, joints and marrow; it judges the thoughts and attitudes of the heart.*
>
> —HEBREWS 4:12

2. *Choose joyful thoughts.* It is so important to remember that joy is a choice, not a feeling! Satan can't steal your joy unless you let him.

Rejoice in the Lord always. I will say it again: Rejoice!
—PHILIPPIANS 4:4

3. *Fix your eyes on Jesus.* You will always see more clearly if you simply take your eyes off yourself and place them on Jesus!

> *Let us fix our eyes on Jesus, the author and perfecter of our faith.*
> —HEBREWS 12:2

4. *Let God fight your battles.* God is stronger, wiser, and more able to fight. Sometimes He just wants you to be still and watch Him go to work on your behalf!

> *The Lord will fight for you; you need only to be still.*
> —EXODUS 14:14

5. *Enjoy the moment you're in.* Realize that every thought that dwells on yesterday keeps you from enjoying today. You can't experience the abundance of God's grace for today, if you're still stuck in yesterday!

> *But seek first His kingdom and His righteousness, and all these things will be given to you as well. Therefore do not worry about tomorrow, for tomorrow will worry about itself. Each day has enough trouble of its own.*
> —MATTHEW 6:33–34

Pray It Through

Dear Father God, I pray that You will release me from the trouble of yesterday and give me strength for today. Please help me focus my thoughts on You, Your wisdom, Your purpose, and Your plan. May I let go of my agenda and cling to Your promises! May I allow You to be God in and through every situation I face! Please help me to put these five principals to work so that I can be more victorious in my thought life.

> *No man has the mind of Christ, except him who makes it his business to obey him.*
> —GEORGE MACDONALD

AND THE PEACE OF GOD, WHICH TRANSCENDS ALL UNDERSTANDING WILL GUARD YOUR HEARTS AND YOUR MINDS IN CHRIST JESUS

Phil 4:7

Day 10

MINDFULLY MOVING FORWARD

In Your unfailing love You will lead the people You have redeemed. In Your strength You will guide them to Your holy dwelling.

—EXODUS 15:13

Live It Out

The Lord's great love is yours. You do not have to be consumed by thoughts of what you could have done better in the years that have passed. The Lord loves you today, and He wants to see how you will use this day to glorify Him. How will you make a difference today? You don't have to be the next big rocket scientist, the next Billy Graham, or even the next big Christian music artist. God is calling you to be you! The best you that you can be!

What does that mean for you? How will you determine to put your best foot forward starting today? Do you have a dream in your heart, a desire to do something for God, or maybe something lingering from your days that have passed? It's not too late to get started! God has given you today! Press the Reset button, and move forward.

Forgetting what is behind and straining toward what is ahead, I press on toward the goal to win the prize for which God has called me heavenward in Christ Jesus.

—PHILIPPIANS 3:13-14

Pray It Through

Dear Father God, thank You for giving me the opportunity to forget about yesterday and it's many issues. I look forward to what You have for me today and press on in You. I will keep my eyes fixed on the prize that You have waiting for me in heaven. I will move forward knowing that great things are in store for me!

> *No one who really wants to count for God can afford to play at Christianity.*
>
> —H. A. IRONSIDE

Day 11

FAITH MINDED

If the Lord delights in a man's way, He makes his steps firm; though he stumble, he will not fall, for the Lord upholds him with His hand.

—PSALM 37:23-24

Live It Out

I watched a great display of childlike faith when my family was here to visit. My nephew Andrew has managed to teach me many lessons of my Father in heaven through his seven years of life.

He would jump from the edge of the pool into his dad's arms. He had little floaties on his arms to keep him afloat. Yet I watched Andrew say these words to his dad, "Come closer, Daddy." Andrew wanted to make sure that his dad would be there to catch him when he jumped. Dustin reassured him and let him know that he would be there. Dustin didn't move closer; he didn't argue with his son, but he simply let him know that he would catch him when he jumped, and he did exactly that.

I often have similar questions for my Father in heaven. Lord, will you catch me? Do you mind coming a bit closer? Lord, will your hands catch me when I fall? O Lord, can you help me with this next leap of faith? Life is filled with wonder, and many times I find myself taking leaps into my Father's arms. Often during the jump, I can't see His hands. I'm jumping blindly into the hands that hold me fast— hands that have never let me down. I jump knowing that God is faithful! I jump trusting in His promises. I jump knowing that God has never given me a reason to doubt His love.

Is there an area of your life that you need to trust God with? Are you ready to jump? Do you know that God will be there to catch you? He cares deeply for you and will never let you down! Feel free to jump into the arms that promise to sustain you.

But now, this is what the Lord says—He who created you, O Jacob, He who formed you, O Israel: "Fear not, for I have redeemed you; I have summoned you by name; you are mine. When you pass through the waters, I will be with you; and when you pass through the rivers, they will not sweep over you. When you walk through the fire, you will not be burned; the flames will not set you ablaze. For I am the Lord, your God, the Holy One of Israel, your Savior."

—ISAIAH 43:1-3

Pray It Through

Dear Abba, I trust in Your unfailing love. You have been there to catch me time and again. I know that I need not fear anything in life, for You will be the One to comfort and guide me. I trust You with my life and freely jump into the arms that hold me fast. Thank You for Your tremendous faithfulness in my life!

Is prayer your steering wheel or spare tire?
—CORRIE TEN BOOM

Day 12

CHILDLIKE MINDSET

*Simply let your "Yes" be "Yes," and your "No," "No";
anything beyond this comes from the evil one.*

—MATTHEW 5:37

Live It Out

My little nephew has been learning this verse. My sister noticed that Andrew would change his mind a lot, so she decided to teach him this verse. Here's his version,

"Let your yes be yes, let your no be no."

Even at the precious age of five, Andrew is learning how to be a man of his word. I think this is a very important lesson that we can learn. How often do we lack the follow through we need? How often do we fall short on finishing what we start? Let's take a deeper look into this passage. What is God trying to show us?

> *And don't say anything you don't mean. This counsel is embedded deep in our traditions. You only make things worse when you lay down a smoke screen of pious talk, saying, "I'll pray for you," and never doing it, or saying, "God be with you," and not meaning it. You don't make*

your words true by embellishing them with religious lace. In making your speech sound more religious, it becomes less true. Just say "yes" and "no." When you manipulate words to get your own way, you go wrong.

—MATTHEW 5:33-37 (MSG)

It's rather simple. Don't you think. Just like Andrew says, "Let your yes be yes, let your no be no." No explanation needed—if only we live out what we say we will do!

Pray It Through

Dear Father God, I pray that I will be a man/woman of my word. Please show me where I have lacked the discipline to follow through on something I said I would do. Help me to daily examine my actions!

> *Maturity starts with the willingness to give oneself.*
> —ELISABETH ELLIOT

Day 13

RESISTING THE DEVIL

Submit yourselves, then, to God. Resist the devil, and he will flee from you.

—JAMES 4:7

Live It Out

The devil knows how powerful your mind can be if focused on Christ. He knows that you're a threat to him if all your thoughts are lined up with God's Word, so he will attack. I can guarantee you that. The first place he attacks is your mind. If he can get your thoughts off of God, then he can take you anywhere. He will drag you through the mud and beat you up if you let him. But you can experience freedom if you simply submit yourself to God and resist the devil.

Do not—and I repeat do not—let the devil pester you! God is the authority over your life, and you don't ever have to take what Satan tries to dish out. Do exactly what the Scripture says, "Resist the devil, and he will flee from you." Do not entertain thoughts that Satan may bring saying, "You're not good enough," "You should have done this better," "If you were only like so and so," "You need to be a better Christian," etc. Don't let Satan beat you up; instead, let God build you up!

VICTORIOUS MINDSET | DAY 13

The thief comes to steal and kill and destroy; I have come that they may have life, and have it to the full.

—JOHN 10:10

Pray It Through

Dear Father God, today I choose to resist every ugly thought that the enemy tries to plant in my mind. I want my thoughts to dwell on Your goodness, Your faithfulness, and Your purpose for my life. Please give me the strength to resist my enemy today and experience the full and abundant life You offer.

And Satan trembles when he sees, the weakest saint upon his knees.

—WILLIAM COWPER

Day 14

DRAWING NEAR TO GOD

Come near to God and He will come near to you ...

—JAMES 4:8

Live It Out

This is great news! You see, Satan wants to be a roadblock between you and God. He will say and do whatever it takes to keep you from having a vibrant relationship with the Lord. This is why you have to resist Satan. Make him flee so you can draw near to God. God wants to be as near to you as possible. Will you draw near to Him? It's a direct path. You don't have to cut any corners. It's not a maze you have to find your way through. God wants you to just come near and He will be right there to come near to you.

Wash your hands, you sinners, and purify your hearts, you double-minded.

—JAMES 4:8

God desires our submission. He wants us to resist the devil so we can draw near to Him. Then comes this part of scripture that reminds us we struggle daily with sin. We can never take sin lightly. We must stay on guard and wash our hands of the sin that creeps into our lives. We must purify our hearts before the Lord daily. God doesn't want us to say we desire to live for Him then turn around and live for the world. He wants all or nothing. Choose to give Him your all today!

Let us then approach the throne of grace with confidence, so that we may receive mercy and find grace to help us in our time of need.

—HEBREWS 4:16

Pray It Through

Dear Father God, I submit my life to You. I continue to resist the devil and all his schemes. May I draw near to You daily and enjoy the nearness of You in my life. Please help me to see if there is anything unclean in my heart and help me to purify myself before You. Thank You that I can approach Your throne of grace with confidence and experience the full measure of Your mercy on a daily basis!

We are not only to renounce evil, but to manifest the truth. We tell people the world is vain; let our lives manifest that it is so. We tell them that our home is above and that all these things are transitory. Does our dwelling look like it? O to live consistent lives!

—JAMES HUDSON TAYLOR

Day 15

DEALING WITH DISTRACTIONS

Do not love the world or anything in the world. If anyone loves the world, the love of the Father is not in him. For everything in the world—the cravings of sinful man, the lust of his eyes and the boasting of what he has and does—comes not from the Father but from the world. The world and its desires pass away, but the man who does the will of God lives forever.

—1 JOHN 2:15-17

Live It Out

I really love this passage of Scripture. I love that the author, John, doesn't beat around the bush. He gets straight to the point. I learn best from those who get straight to the point, so I greatly appreciate John's approach.

My husband and I decided to apply this passage of Scripture to our own lives. We decided to keep the television off for a month. We wanted to take time to recognize that it can be a distraction for us and often it takes away from the quality of life that we so desire to share with each other. It was great to keep the television off. We found ourselves being creative, taking a few more walks, and

VICTORIOUS MINDSET | DAY 15

enjoying a few more talks. It was so nice to have a vacation away from the distracting noise of the TV.

The main reason we did this was to focus on cleansing our minds. We both want to have the mind of Christ (Philippians 2:5). We want to empty ourselves of this world's standards. We want more of God. We want to live lives that are pleasing to God and show that we value the time we have been given.

Is there something in your life that distracts you from spending quality time with those you care about? Is there something in your life that distracts you from quality time with God? Take time this week to seriously look at the distractions in your life and ask God to help you remove them. Let's draw near to God and watch what He can do when we are fully surrendered to His purpose. May the world and its desires slowly fade from view as we focus on Christ and all that He has for us.

> *Do not be conformed to this world (this age), [fashioned after and adapted to its external, superficial customs], but be transformed (changed) by the [entire] renewal of your mind [by its new ideals and its new attitude], so that you may prove [for yourselves] what is the good and acceptable and perfect will of God, even the thing which is good and acceptable and perfect [in His sight for you].*
>
> —ROMANS 12:2 (AMP)

VICTORIOUS MINDSET | DAY 15

Pray It Through

Dear Father God, I pray that You will help me identify the many distractions in my life. Please show me where I am wasting my time and not completely living my life for Your glory. I pray that this world and its desires will slowly fade from my view, as I focus on all that You have for me.

> *If Christ does not reign over the mundane events in our lives, He does not reign at all.*
>
> —PAUL TRIPP

Day 16

NO WORRIES

But blessed is the man who trusts in the Lord, whose confidence is in Him. He will be like a tree planted by the water that sends out its roots by the stream. It does not fear when heat comes; its leaves are always green. It has no worries in a year of drought and never fails to bear fruit.

—JEREMIAH 17:7–8

Live It Out

I love the imagery that this verse brings to life in my mind. I want to be that tree planted by the water. I want to have this kind of confidence in the Lord.

I want my roots to go down deep into the soil of God's grace. I want my life to exhibit a state of fruitfulness that comes from staying attached to the Vine of Life (John 15:5). I want my mind to produce thoughts that are pleasing to the Lord. I desire to place my worries behind me and live by faith as I move forward in life.

I will be blessed as I place my full confidence, my full attention, and all my thoughts on the Lord. I can trust God and know that He has my best interest in mind. I can place my full confidence in His promises and know that He will never fail me. I'm blessed when

I choose to trust in God's unfailing love and remember that He is always faithful!

> *Trust in the Lord with all your heart and lean not on your own understanding; in all your ways acknowledge Him, and He will make your paths straight.*
> —PROVERBS 3:5-6

Pray It Through

Dear Father God, I pray that I will be this tree planted by the water. May I continue to place my full trust and confidence in You. I know that Your Word is true. I know that You will never fail me. I know that You will always be faithful. I pray that even in the driest times of my life, I will produce fruit for the kingdom! May the branches of my life truly lift up to honor You!

> *I believe the Bible is the best gift God has ever given to man. All the good from the Savior of the world is communicated to us through this book.*
> —PRESIDENT ABRAHAM LINCOLN

Day 17

SWAN-LIKE ATTITUDE

As water reflects a face, so a man's heart reflects the man.
—PROVERBS 27:19

Live It Out

I love watching swans' float. They are so graceful and their reflection in the water is a reminder of what Proverbs 27:19 entails. Am I reflecting the Father in my thoughts, my words, and my actions? If not, what needs to change? How can I better reflect the One who knows me, who sees me, who loves me? How can I better reflect the work done on the cross for me?

A swan always looks so delicate and perfect to me. It simply floats along. It's not distracted by what others are thinking or the pictures often taken. It just simply floats along. Sometimes, I feel like I need to do a little more floating. I need to rest a little more and relax in all that God is. I get so worked up and so distracted that I forget to float. I forget the elegance of simply being in the Lord's presence.

So this week, I choose to float. I choose to grace the waters with a swan like attitude. I will not be distracted by the storms that come. I will allow God's peace to rest securely in my heart. I will live knowing that God's peace truly does surpass my understanding. He's got great things in store for me and I will rest in this. I will float on the waters of God's love and treasure the moments of elegance in His abundant grace!

> *From the fullness of His grace we have all received one blessing after another.*
>
> —JOHN 1:16

Pray It Through

Dear Father God, I choose to float in Your grace this week. Help me to remember that I am a child of God, loved and cherished by the King of kings. Please help me to not get distracted by the things of this world. I pray my heart will be steadfast on You and that I may reflect the glory of my King!

> *Let us never forget that what we are is more important than what we do.*
>
> —JAMES HUDSON TAYLOR

PLAN OF ACTION

Therefore, prepare your minds for action; be self controlled; set your hope fully on the grace to be given you when Jesus Christ is revealed. As obedient children, do not conform to the evil desires you had when you lived in ignorance. But just as He who called you is holy, so be holy in all you do; for it is written: "Be holy, because I am holy."

—1 PETER 1:13–16

The Plan of Action

1. **Prepare.** Today is a new day. Set aside the things of yesterday and resolve to be actively involved in God-size tasks today.

2. **Practice self-control.** Don't be irrational or out of control. Let your hope be in the One whose mercy has been poured out on you in abundance. Then share that with those you come in contact with today.

3. **Plan.** Be obedient. Live a holy life. To the best of your ability, choose wisely today. Make decisions that will impact eternity in a positive way. Remember, you only get to live today once!

You, therefore, must be perfect [growing into complete maturity of godliness in mind and character, having reached the proper height of virtue and integrity], as your heavenly Father is perfect.

—MATTHEW 5:48 (AMP)

Pray It Through

Lord, please prepare my mind to be actively involved in all the moments You've created for me today. Help me to practice self-control in everything I do as I remember I'm a reflection of You everywhere I go. May I continually become more obedient to You and Your desires for my life. Please melt away anything in me that is not holy and help me to become more Christlike with every step I take.

> *Spiritual strongholds begin with a thought. One thought becomes a consideration. A consideration develops into an attitude, which leads then to action. Action repeated becomes a habit, and a habit establishes a "power base for the enemy," that is, a stronghold.*
>
> —ELISABETH ELLIOT

Day 19

LIVING COMPLETE

Be perfect, therefore, as your heavenly Father is perfect.
—MATTHEW 5:48

Live It Out

This verse can be quite intimidating, if you do not know the meaning of the word perfect. I mean, how many people do you know that have achieved perfection on this earth? Yikes, I have to say I haven't found any, and I myself have quite a few imperfections. That's why it is so important to look into what the word perfect means.

What is the context of this verse? What is Jesus calling us to do when He calls us to a life of perfection? Well, let's take a look into the Greek meaning of the word perfect.

The word perfect in the Greek means "finished, wanting nothing, and complete." All right, that doesn't sound so bad. Let's place that in the verse and see how it sounds.

Be complete, therefore, as your heavenly Father is complete.

Wow, a life of completeness. Now that sounds like the kind of life I want to live! A life complete in Jesus is a life filled with promise and meaning. Will you follow the One who offers a life of completeness?

You have made known to me the path of life; You will fill me with joy in Your presence, with eternal pleasures at Your right hand.

—PSALM 16:11

Pray It Through

O Lord, how I long to have the complete, full, and abundant life You offer in Your Word. Please help my mind to be fixed on Your Truth. May my thoughts dwell on Your goodness, may I follow You with every step I take, and may my mind steadily chase after the things of You.

Learn to say "no" to the good so you can say "yes" to the best.
—JOHN C. MAXWELL

Day 20

THE COMPLETE LIFE

What does a life complete in Jesus mean?

1. It means no more worrying about tomorrow.

> *Therefore do not worry about tomorrow, for tomorrow will worry about itself. Each day has enough trouble of its own.*
>
> —MATTHEW 6:34

2. It means no more searching for the answers.

> *Jesus answered, "I am the way and the truth and the life. No one comes to the Father except through Me."*
>
> —JOHN 14:6

3. It means you're adopted to the family of God.

> *To redeem them that were under the law, that we might receive the adoption of sons.*
>
> —GALATIANS 4:5 (KJV)

4. It means peace during the storms in life.

Fear not, for I have redeemed you; I have summoned you by name; you are mine. When you pass through the waters, I will be with you; and when you pass through the rivers, they will not sweep over you. When you walk through the fire, you will not be burned; the flames will not set you ablaze.

—ISAIAH 43:1–2

5. It means I'm loved for who I am, not what I can do.

For it is by grace you have been saved, through faith— and this is not from yourselves, it is the gift of God— not by works, so that no one can boast.

—EPHESIANS 2:8–9

6. It means someone has a plan for me; my days will be filled with adventure.

"For I know the plans I have for you," declares the Lord, "plans to prosper you and not to harm you, plans to give you hope and a future."

—JEREMIAH 29:11

7. It means there will always be someone in my life who will not fail me.

Blessed is he whose help is the God of Jacob, whose hope is in the Lord his God, the Maker of heaven and earth, the sea and everything in them—the Lord, who remains faithful forever.

—PSALM 146:5–6

8. It's a life filled with promise and possibility.

> *Not that I have already obtained all this, or have already been made perfect, but I press on to take hold of that for which Christ Jesus took hold of me. Brothers, I do not consider myself yet to have taken hold of it. But one thing I do: Forgetting what is behind and straining toward what is ahead, I press on toward the goal to win the prize for which God has called me heavenward in Christ Jesus.*
>
> —PHILIPPIANS 3:12–14

9. It means all things will eventually work out for good in my life.

> *And we know that in all things God works for the good of those who love him, who have been called according to his purpose.*
>
> —ROMANS 8:28

10. Most of all, it means forgiveness for my sins and a love that forgets.

> *For as high as the heavens are above the earth, so great is his love for those who fear him; as far as the east is from the west, so far has he removed our transgressions from us.*
>
> —PSALM 103:11–12

VICTORIOUS MINDSET | DAY 20

Pray It Through

Dear Father God, thank You for giving me a complete life through Your Son, Jesus Christ. Honestly, thank You does not seem adequate enough for all that You have given me. I pray that my life will be lived out in a way that says thank You every day. May my life be honoring to You and may I always seek to glorify You! Help me to live the complete life through Your Son Jesus Christ!

> *Every time we pray our horizon is altered, our attitude to things is altered, not sometimes but every time, and the amazing thing is that we don't pray more.*
> —OSWALD CHAMBERS

Day 21

SHARPENED BY THE WORD

Your word is a lamp to my feet and a light for my path.
—PSALM 119:105

Live It Out

The above verse tells us that the Word of God is a lamp to our feet and light to our path. God's Word lights our path. It gives us guidance and direction. It teaches us how to walk uprightly and how to align our thoughts with God's thinking. Our minds are constantly being bombarded by this world's standards. There is only one way to fight back and that is through the Word of God.

> *For the Word of God is living and active. Sharper than any double-edged sword, it penetrates even to dividing soul and spirit, joints and marrow; it judges the thoughts and attitudes of the heart.*
>
> —HEBREWS 4:12

The Word of God is active. It sharpens us daily when we read it and put it into practice. It prepares us for the battles we face and gives us the strength to fight victoriously. Your sword for battle can only stay sharpened if you take time to sharpen it. Look at a knife in your knife set. They too need to be sharpened. How much more does your sword in the Spirit need to be sharpened, as it is used daily? Will you stay sharp for the Lord?

May those who fear You rejoice when they see me, for I have put my hope in your Word.

—PSALM 119:74

Pray It Through

Dear Father God, I pray I will never take for granted the opportunity I have to read Your Word freely. Help me to appreciate the freedom that I have in this country to read the Word of God, memorize it, and apply it. I pray for my brothers and sisters in other countries who have had this right taken from them. I pray a hedge of protection around them and pray You will continue to light their path. May the words they have memorized continue to come to life for them!

> *I would sooner read five lines of the Bible than hear five masses in the "Church."*
>
> —ANNE ASKEW
> (martyred for her faith at Smithfield in 1545)

Day 22

WORRY FREE

Then Jesus said to His disciples: "Therefore I tell you, do not worry about your life, what you will eat; or about your body, what you will wear. Life is more than food, and the body more than clothes. Consider the ravens: They do not sow or reap, they have no storeroom or barn; yet God feeds them. And how much more valuable you are than birds! Who of you by worrying can add a single hour to his life?"

—LUKE 12:22–25

Live It Out

I love how Jesus can go from a story about a rich fool to this passage above. He goes from someone who has everything to someone who is worrying about their next meal. He stops us in our tracks and reminds us to look around. We need to see how God is providing for the birds of the air and the flowers of the field. The bird mentioned above is the raven. The raven was considered an unclean bird and therefore had little value to the people of that day.

God cared for this little raven, even though it was an unclean bird, a bird that had no ability to store up its own food. It was fully dependent on God. If God cares this much for a little bird, how much more does He care for us and will He provide for us?

The passage of Scripture goes into a question, "Who can add a single hour to his life by worrying?" Have you ever gained time by worrying about tomorrow? Or have you lost time by looking to your future and forgetting to enjoy the present? It's time to stop borrowing trouble! Let's hand our worries over to God. Let's find out what He can do when our lives are fully surrendered to Him.

> *But seek first His kingdom and His righteousness, and all these things will be given to you as well. Therefore do not worry about tomorrow, for tomorrow will worry about itself. Each day has enough trouble of its own.*
>
> —MATTHEW 6:33-34

Pray It Through

Dear Father God, You know the things that are on my heart. The things that cause me pain. The things that cause me to fret. I lift them up to You right now, right here. I pray that You will make things right in my life, that You will set things straight. I know I can depend on You. I do not have to worry about tomorrow because You have said You will take care of it. I trust You with my whole life. I trust in Your plans for me and all Your promises! May You continue Your good work inside of me! Thank You, Lord!

> *It is not the body's posture, but the heart's attitude that counts when we pray.*
>
> —BILLY GRAHAM

Day 23

GOD'S VIEW ON LIFE

"For My thoughts are not your thoughts, neither are your ways My ways," declares the Lord.

—ISAIAH 55:8

Live It Out

This passage of Scripture tends to make a lot of sense to me. I don't have to dig too deep or look into it too heavily to understand it. I've lived it! I've seen that God's thoughts are much different than my own. His ways are certainly much different than my ways! I'm very grateful for this most days. Yes, I did say most days. I have days where I do not understand what God is doing or why we differ so much on how things should be done. I guess sometimes I just want to be clued in! Can you identify with that thought?

The truth is many of us want in on what God is thinking. We want to know what the plan is and how things are going to work out. We're kind of like children in that way because we ask a lot of questions. Sometimes we get answers, but most of the time we don't. It's so important to remember that God's perspective on our life is a lot different. Let's look at the next portion of Scripture in Isaiah.

VICTORIOUS MINDSET | DAY 23

As the heavens are higher than the earth, so are my ways higher than Your ways and my thoughts than Your thoughts.
—ISAIAH 55:9

God knows how to handle tomorrow. He knows how to embrace today. He knows how to forgive the mistakes of yesterday. He knows how to prepare for the future. He knows how to love your children. He knows how to love your spouse. He knows how to love the unlovable. He knows how to help you do your best at your job. He knows about your finances. He knows how to heal your body. He knows virtually everything that is causing you pain. He will not leave you. He will not fail you. He will always love you!

So please don't worry if you don't have everything figured out because there is One who has it all under control. Hang on to the One who is unchanging! Remain in His steadfast love and rest in the fact that His thoughts are higher than yours!

Find rest, O my soul, in God alone; my hope comes from Him. He alone is my rock and my salvation; He is my fortress, I will not be shaken.

—PSALM 62:5-6

Pray It Through

Dear Father God, thank You that I can just be me. I don't have to have everything figured out. I don't have to be in control. I can look at life as an adventure knowing that You're in control. Thank You for sending Your Son to give me purpose, meaning, and True Life. I'm so blessed to believe in Someone who knows my thoughts better than I do. Help me to carry out Your ways!

VICTORIOUS MINDSET | DAY 23

Many Christians have what we might call a "cultural holiness." They adapt to the character and behavior pattern of Christians around them. As the Christian culture around them is more or less holy, so these Christians are more or less holy. But God has not called us to be like those around us. He has called us to be like himself. Holiness is nothing less than conformity to the character of God.

—JERRY BRIDGES

CHANGE
YOUR
thoughts
AND YOU'LL
change
YOUR
WORLD

Day 24

THOUGHT INVENTORY

You were taught, with regard to your former way of life, to put off your old self, which is being corrupted by its deceitful desires; to be made new in the attitude of your minds; and to put on the new self, created to be like God in true righteousness and holiness.

—EPHESIANS 4:22–24

Live It Out

God's Truth reminds us that we no longer live in our old sinful nature. We have to let go of it for something far greater, something only God can give. This new life comes with a new attitude—a changing of our minds! What will our attitudes look like towards Christ? Will we develop a mind of Christ and reflect the character we have seen lived out in our Savior?

I know what my thought inventory is, and when I look over it, I see what needs to change. Every once in a while I get off track and allow negative thoughts to occupy my inventory list. I need to take that space back. There can only be room for thoughts that are pleasing to God.

What are the things that cause you to not be as focused? Can you give them up for a little while? Let's take a little more time in the Word, in prayer, in worship, in nature, and even spend time listening. Let's get our minds focused on Christ and reflect His character a little more! Our thoughts do matter!

> *And this is my prayer: that your love may abound more and more in knowledge and depth of insight, so that you may be able to discern what is best and may be pure and blameless until the day of Christ, filled with the fruit of righteousness that comes through Jesus Christ—to the glory and praise of God.*
>
> PHILIPPIANS 1:9-11

Pray It Through

Lord, please help me to discern what is best. May I not allow a single thought of negativity or filth to occupy my mind. May I daily renew my mind in Your Word and saturate it with Your Truth. May Your Truth take up residence in my heart so that there is no room for fear, doubt, or anxiety! May my thoughts be honoring to You!

> *No one can sum up all God is able to accomplish through one solitary life, wholly yielded, adjusted, and obedient to Him.*
>
> —D. L. MOODY

Day 25

CAPTIVE FOR CHRIST

[Inasmuch as we] refute arguments and theories and reasonings and every proud and lofty thing that sets itself up against the [true] knowledge of God; and we lead every thought and purpose away captive into the obedience of Christ (the Messiah, the Anointed One).

—2 CORINTHIANS 10:5 (AMP)

Live It Out

This verse reminds us that we need to take our thoughts captive daily. We cannot dwell on things that are negative or that don't please the Lord. We need to make every thought obedient to Jesus Christ. This should not happen when we feel like it, but it should be happening daily—every moment of our lives.

I have been studying this verse a lot, and I can tell you it's rewarding to take every thought captive. I have noticed the difference it is making in my life to truly allow God to help me see His Truth. I'm not dwelling on things that aren't true. I'm not assuming things from what people say or allowing Satan to twist what someone says. We have to remember that we can't change anyone else, but we can change how we respond, react, and receive from others. We can learn how to live from God's Truth!

VICTORIOUS MINDSET | DAY 25

Therefore, since Christ suffered in His body, arm yourselves also with the same attitude, because He who has suffered in His body is done with sin.

—1 PETER 4:1

Pray It Through

Dear Father God, thank You for continuing to show me how important it is to have the mind of Christ. I know that every thought I think is important to You. My thoughts can lead me down a road of righteousness or a road of unrighteousness. I choose the road of righteousness. I choose the road that leads to life. Help me to think more purely and honestly.

Help my thoughts reflect Your Character. I pray for this cleansing of my mind and that You will renew it daily. Please arm me with the same attitude that Christ had, that I may be more effective and productive for Your kingdom!

> *We must assess our thoughts and beliefs and reckon whether they are moving us closer to conformity to Christ or farther away from it.*
>
> —JOHN ORTBERG

Day 26

PEACE OF MIND

You will keep in perfect peace him whose mind is steadfast, because he trusts in You.

—ISAIAH 26:3

Live It Out

The way to obtain perfect peace is to keep our minds on Christ. The only way to keep our minds steadfast on God's work is through His Word. We must renew our minds daily and wash them with the Word of God. The world will continue to bombard you with it's thoughts and ideas for you. You can overcome it all by reading God's Word and applying it.

You, dear children, are from God and have overcome them, because the One who is in you is greater than the one who is in the world.

—1 JOHN 4:4

We overcome this world by setting our minds on Christ. We must remember that the One who lives inside of us is greater than the one who lives in this world. We have the power to overcome every scheme of the enemy by keeping our minds cleansed by God's Word.

VICTORIOUS MINDSET | DAY 26

Those who live according to the sinful nature have their minds set on what that nature desires; but those who live in accordance with the Spirit have their minds set on what the Spirit desires. The mind of sinful man is death, but the mind controlled by the Spirit is life and peace.

—ROMANS 8:5-6

Pray It Through

Lord, I desire to live according to the Spirit and have my mind fixed on the things of You. Please control my mind by the power of Your Holy Spirit and enable me to have this mind set on life and peace in You! I pray that my mind will be a tool for You and You alone!

Blessed are the single-hearted, for they shall enjoy much peace. If you refuse to be hurried and pressed, if you stay your soul on God, nothing can keep you from that clearness of spirit which is life and peace. In that stillness you know what His will is.

—AMY CARMICHAEL

Day 27

HANDING OVER THE PAINTBRUSH

Forgetting what is behind and straining toward what is ahead, I press on toward the goal to win the prize for which God has called me heavenward in Christ Jesus.
—PHILIPPIANS 3:13-14

Live It Out

This is one of my favorite verses! I love that I'm called to forget what lies behind me. Yesterday can only trip me up if I let it. I make the choice daily to start fresh with a clean slate. God's mercies are new for me each morning. What an amazing thought! I don't have to live on yesterday's mercies, and I don't have to wallow in all that wasn't accomplished. Today is a new day, and God has something beautiful in store for it

Through the Lord's mercies we are not consumed, because His compassions fail not. They are new every morning; Great is Your faithfulness.
—LAMENTATIONS 3:22-23 (NKJV)

Every time I watch a sunset, I'm reminded of this. As the sun sets and gives way to the night, painting its brilliant colors in the sky, I'm reminded that tomorrow is a new day with new colors that God wants to paint into my life. I've never seen the same sunset twice. In that I mean the colors of each sunset are vastly different—just like my life! The colors of today come out in different ways. Every day I'm a brand-new canvas for the Lord to paint His marvelous work in!

> *From the rising of the sun to the place where it sets, the name of the Lord is to be praised.*
>
> —PSALM 113:3

Pray It Through

Dear Father God, thank You so much for giving me new mercies every morning! I look forward to the colors You will paint in my life today, so as I say this I hand the paint brush over to You! I know You will be faithful to paint a masterpiece with my life!

> *Each one of us is God's special work of art. Through us, He teaches and inspires, delights and encourages, informs and uplifts all those who view our lives. God, the master artist, is most concerned about expressing Himself—His thoughts and His intentions—through what He paints in our character. [He] wants to paint a beautiful portrait of His Son in and through your life. A painting like no other in all of time.*
>
> —JONI EARECKSON TADA

Day 28

NO ONE LOVES YOU MORE

If God is for us, who can be against us?

—ROMANS 8:31

Live It Out

This is an amazing statement. There is no one bigger than God, no one who can fight harder than God, no one who has more strength than God, no one who has more answers than God, no one who knows you better than God, and certainly no one who will be there longer for you than God.

There is no one who will go to bat for you like God, no one who can love you more than God, no one who cares about your needs more, no one who sees your pain more, and no one who has the power to heal you more. There is no one like God!

God is for you! He will always be for you, and because of this, you never have to fear those who may come against you. Stand strong in the Lord. This is the day of victory in Jesus!

> *The Lord your God is with you, He is mighty to save. He will take great delight in you, He will quiet you with His love, He will rejoice over you with singing.*
>
> —ZEPHANIAH 3:17

VICTORIOUS MINDSET | DAY 28

Pray It Through

Oh Lord, how good it is to know that You are for me. Truly no weapon formed against me will prosper. Your strength can overcome my strongest opponent. Your love can enable me to stand on the heights of despair. Your arms of strength can embrace my weary soul and melt away the hopelessness my heart feels. Your love, O Lord, is greater than the highest mountain and deeper than the deepest ocean. May my mind dwell on these things as I live in the abundance of Your love today!

> *We should be astonished at the goodness of God, stunned that He should bother to call us by name, our mouths wide open at His love, bewildered that at this very moment we are standing on holy ground.*
> —BRENNAN MANNING

Day 29

LAVISHED ON ME

How great is the love the Father has lavished on us, that we should be called children of God!

—1 JOHN 3:1

Live It Out

God continues to pour out His love in abundance on my life. He continues to shape me and mold me into all that He desires me to be. He doesn't say, "He'll love me when I'm good enough." He doesn't say, "He'll love me when I stop falling." He doesn't say, "He'll love me when I stop being selfish." He doesn't put a price tag on His love. He doesn't make me work for it. He simply loves me. What an astounding thought. God's love has no measure! His love is vast, and He truly lavishes it upon us. Wow, what a beautiful picture! I can't help but smile thinking about it.

When I said, "My foot is slipping," Your love, O Lord, supported me.

—PSALM 94:18

God's love is there to catch me when I fall. He is there to support me. He is there to lift me up. His love will always hold me steady.

VICTORIOUS MINDSET | DAY 29

"Though the mountains be shaken and the hills be removed, yet My unfailing love for you will not be shaken nor My covenant of peace be removed," says the Lord, who has compassion on you.

—ISAIAH 54:10

God's love is unfailing. This is so powerful. Mountains and hills will give way, but God's love will never fail! He will stay true—God will never turn His back on you!

The Lord your God is with you, He is mighty to save. He will take great delight in you, He will quiet you with His love, He will rejoice over you with singing.

—ZEPHANIAH 3:17

God will quiet your fears, your anxieties, your troubles, and everything you face with His love. He will always be with you and take great delight in who you are as you surrender your life to Him!

And I pray that you, being rooted and established in love, may have power, together with all the saints, to grasp how wide and long and high and deep is the love of Christ, and to know this love that surpasses knowledge—that you may be filled to the measure of all the fullness of God.

—EPHESIANS 3:17–19

God's love is measureless. We can't begin to fathom how big His love is for us. We will never be able to comprehend how much God loves us. His love will always be enough.

This is how God showed His love among us: He sent his one and only Son into the world that we might live through

him. This is love: not that we loved God, but that He loved us and sent His Son as an atoning sacrifice for our sins.
—1 JOHN 4:9-10

Pray It Through

Dear Father God, Your love still amazes me! I get off track pretty often, but You are always there to put my feet back on the Solid Rock. You have never failed me. Your love has always lifted me up and helped me soar through every detail of life. I'm so grateful that Your Son made it possible for me to experience what true love is and how to express that daily. Thank You for loving me and for never making me work for that love. Thank You for just loving me the way that I am, just as I am, and loving me so much that You help me become something more through Your love! Thank You for helping me have the mindset of Christ that I may live a more full and abundant life.

> *God proved His love on the Cross. When Christ hung, and bled, and died, it was God saying to the world, "I love you."*
> —BILLY GRAHAM

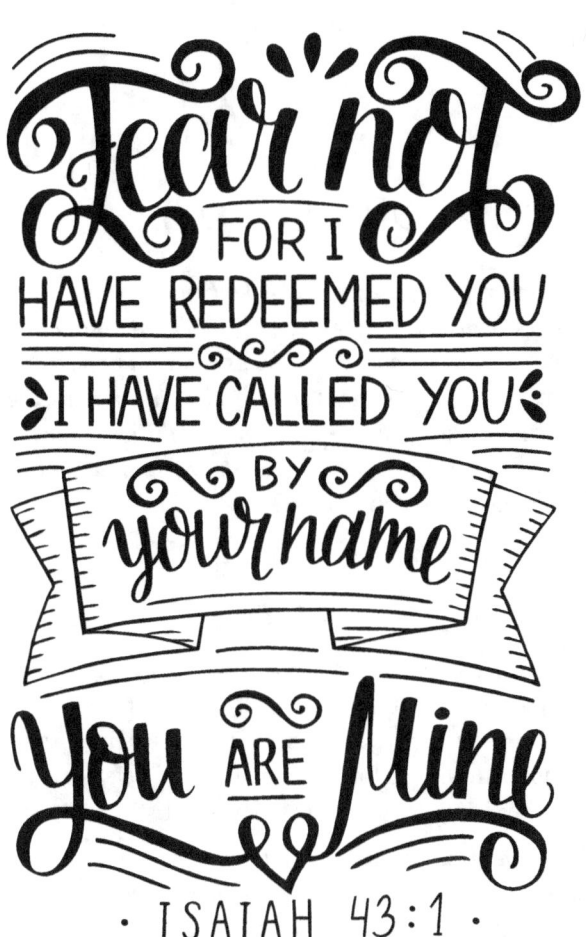

Day 30

VICTORY OR DEFEAT

Therefore, since we are surrounded by such a great cloud of witnesses, let us throw off everything that hinders and the sin that so easily entangles, and let us run with perseverance the race marked out for us. Let us fix our eyes on Jesus, the author and perfecter of our faith, who for the joy set before Him endured the cross, scorning its shame, and sat down at the right hand of the throne of God.

—HEBREWS 12:1–2

Live It Out

There was no greater victory in history than the victory of the cross. God triumphed over death by raising His Son to life. Through this one act, we now can experience victory in our own lives. Today, we have a choice: run with victory in mind or stand defeated. Will you chase after the victory that is yours in Jesus Christ?

It is not the critic who counts: not the man who points out how the strong man stumbles or where the doer of deeds could have done better. The credit belongs to the man who is actually in the arena, whose face is marred by dust and sweat and blood, who strives valiantly, who errs and comes up short again and again, because there is no effort without

error or shortcoming, but who knows the great enthusiasms, the great devotions, who spends himself for a worthy cause; who, at the best, knows, in the end, the triumph of high achievement, and who, at the worst, if he fails, at least he fails while daring greatly, so that his place shall never be with those cold and timid souls who knew neither victory nor defeat.
—THEODORE ROOSEVELT

I'm not saying that I have this all together, that I have it made. But I am well on my way, reaching out for Christ, who has so wondrously reached out for me. Friends, don't get me wrong: By no means do I count myself an expert in all of this, but I've got my eye on the goal, where God is beckoning us onward—to Jesus. I'm off and running, and I'm not turning back.
—PHILIPPIANS 3:12-14 (MSG)

Pray It Through

Dear Father God, I continue to run with my eyes fixed on You. I celebrate every victory I've had and will continue to have through You. Thank You for creating in me a desire to fight and win every battle for You! Lord, please help my mind to be ever fixed on the victory You have given me. May my thoughts not dwell on yesterday or even tomorrow, but may my thoughts dwell on Your goodness, Your faithfulness and Your ability to bring me victory every day of my life because of what Jesus did on my behalf when He died on the cross!

> *No one has the mind of Christ, except him who makes it his business to obey Him.*
> —GEORGE MACDONALD

BIBLIOGRAPHY

"A Quote by Corrie Ten Boom." Goodreads. Accessed October 29, 2014.

"A Quote by John C. Maxwell." Goodreads. Accessed October 29, 2014.

"A Quote by William Cowper." Goodreads. Accessed October 29, 2014.

"Amy Carmichael Quotes." Goodreads. Accessed October 29, 2014.

Bible Gateway. 1. The Steadfastness of Truth—Story of Anne Askew. Accessed October 29, 2014. https://www.biblegateway.com/resources/all-women-bible/Steadfastness-Truth-8212-Story.

Blackaby, Henry T., and Claude V. King. *Experiencing God: How to Live the Full Adventure of Knowing and Doing the Will of God.* Nashville, Tenn.: Broadman & Holman Publishers, 1994.

Blamires, Harry. *The Christian Mind: How Should a Christian Think?* Ann Arbor, Mich.: Servant Books, 1963.

"Charles R. Swindoll Quotes." Charles R. Swindoll Quotes (Author of *The Grace Awakening*). Accessed October 29, 2014. https://www.goodreads.com/author/quotes/5139. Charles_R_Swindoll.

"Discipleship Quotes." Discipleship Quotes. Accessed October 29, 2014. http://www.tentmaker.org/Quotes/discipleshipquotes.htm.

"Elisabeth Elliot Quotes | ChristianQuotes.info." ChristianQuotesinfo. Accessed October 29, 2014. http://www.christianquotes.info/quotes-by-author/elisabeth-elliot-quotes/.

Elliot, Elisabeth. *Let Me Be a Woman: Notes on Womanhood for*

Valerie. Wheaton, Ill.: Tyndale House Publishers, 1976.

"Faith Hall of Fame–Henry (Harry) Allan Ironside." Faith Hall of Fame–Henry (Harry) Allan Ironside. Accessed October 29, 2014. http://www.eaec.org/faithhallfame/harryironside.htm

"Famous Christian Quotes." Famous Christian Quotes. Accessed October 29, 2014. http://www.cobblestoneroad ministry. org/2005_CRM/Famous_ChristianQuotes.html.

"God Proved His Love on the Cross (Billy Graham)." Billy Graham Life and Quotes WORLD CHRISTIAN NEWS RSS. Accessed October 29, 2014.

Graham, Billy. *My Answer*. Garden City, N.Y.: Doubleday, 1960.

"Knowledge." Knowledge Is Indispensable to Christian Life and Service. Accessed October 29, 2014. http://www.jerseygrace. org/GraceLife/quotes/Knowledge.htm.

Lewis, C. S. *Mere Christianity: Comprising The Case for Christianity, Christian Behaviour, and Beyond Personality*. New York: Touchstone, 1996.

"Lincoln's Faith in God." Great American History Lincoln's Faith -. Accessed October 29, 2014.

MacDonald, George. *Unspoken Sermons*. New York: George Routledge, 1873.

Manning, Brennan. *The Ragamuffin Gospel*. Sisters, Or.: Multnomah Publishers, 2000.

"Optimism–Insight for Living Ministries Devotionals." Optimism. Accessed October 29, 2014. http://www.insight.org/resources/devotionals/optimism.html.

Ortberg, John. *The Life You've Always Wanted: Spiritual Disciplines for Ordinary People*. Grand Rapids, Mich.: Zondervan Pub. House, 1997.

"Oswald Chambers Quotes." Oswald Chambers Quotes. Accessed October 29, 2014. http://www.winwisdom.com/quotes/author/oswald-chambers.aspx.

Pink, Arthur Walkington. *The Sovereignty of God*. Grand Rapids: Baker Book House, 1965.

Piper, John. *Don't Waste Your Life*. Wheaton, Ill.: Crossway Books, 2003.

Tada, Joni Eareckson. *Secret Strength: For Those Who Search*. Portland, Or.: Multnomah, 1988.

Taylor, James Hudson. *Days of Blessing in Inland China: An Account of Meetings Held in Shan-Si, Etc*. 3rd ed. London: Morgan & Scott, 1890.

"The Man in the Arena–April 23, 1910–Theodore Roosevelt Speeches–Roosevelt Almanac." The Man in the Arena–April 23, 1910–Theodore Roosevelt Speeches–Roosevelt Almanac. Accessed October 29, 2014.

ABOUT THE AUTHOR

Sarah Malanowski is the Founder of the ministry called *The Priceless Journey*. The Priceless Journey exists to empower women who have been marginalized, exploited, neglected, and abused. Sarah works diligently with a team to create resources that go into the hands of the broken all over our communities. She has a strong passion to see every woman embrace her journey of freedom and become all that God desires her to be. We encourage you to get these resources and share them with the broken in your community because every woman deserves to know that she is truly priceless.

Here are helpful resources that Sarah and her team have developed.

You are Priceless *(*English, Spanish & Chinese*)* Every woman deserves to know that she is priceless. In this booklet read the testimonies of five women, who had a life-transforming encounter with Jesus Christ.

You are an Overcomer—Do you know someone struggling with depression, discouragement, thoughts of suicide, addiction, or domestic abuse? Learn what it means to overcome!

You are Fearless—Do you know anyone who feels trapped? This booklet is extremely helpful for those in the commercial sex industry and victims of human trafficking.

You are Worthy—In this booklet women will learn that being worthy is not based on what they've done but on who they already are. This booklet is especially useful in the Pregnancy Care Centers.

You are Loved—Women everywhere have the desire to be loved whether it's in the pew, the prison, the clubs, or streets. In this booklet you discover the truth is that no one can love you like God.

You are Free—Many women are caught in an endless loop of lies with little awareness that there is something more. In this booklet you will learn that Jesus will set you free! You are not your past.

You are Enough—The message of being enough is embedded—am I strong enough, beautiful enough, smart enough? The truth is these are all masks to hide the real you.

Other resources created by Sarah Malanowski are:

Make Your Moments Count—The gift of motherhood is beautiful yet crazy and exhausting. In this book 20 moms join Sarah to share their adventures and provide encouragement.

Life's Compass for Eternal Treasure—In this book Sarah unpacks Psalm 37 and shows how and where we gain direction for life. Study guide included.

Infused with Joy—Being a leader is a daunting task and often filled with great demand and little reward. Be encouraged and empowered as you read this booklet designed for those in leadership.

All resources can be purchased at **thepricelessjourney.org**

The Priceless Journey now has an app available on both Apple and Android! Simply search *Priceless Journey* to find it. More features will be added soon, but for now, it's a great resource with all our booklets and more to come.

IPHONE   ANDROID

Looking for a Speaker?

Sarah has a way with words. Many audiences have left sharing the impact of her words and how its inspired their freedom journey. Sarah shares from the overflow of the work God has done in her life and invites you into her storyline. She loves talking about Jesus and the abundant life He promises us in John 10:10. When you're looking for a speaker to empower your group in their freedom journey, contact Sarah.

Info@empowered2livefree.org
833.691.4673 ext. 3

www.ingramcontent.com/pod-product-compliance
Lightning Source LLC
Chambersburg PA
CBHW050040080526
44586CB00014B/1392